Pebble® Plus

All About Sharks

Oceanic Whitetip Sharks

A 4D Book

by Jody S. Rake

CAPSTONE PRESS
a capstone imprint

Download the Capstone 4D app!

- Ask an adult to download the Capstone 4D app.

- Scan the cover and stars inside the book for additional content.

When you scan a spread, you'll find fun extra stuff to go with this book! You can also find these things on the web at www.capstone4D.com using the password: whitetip.01556

Pebble Plus is published by Capstone Press,
1710 Roe Crest Drive, North Mankato, Minnesota 56003
www.mycapstone.com

Library of Congress Cataloging-in-Publication Data
Names: Rake, Jody Sullivan, author.
Title: Oceanic whitetip sharks : a 4D book / by Jody S. Rake.
Description: North Mankato, Minnesota : Capstone Press, [2019] | Series: Pebble plus. All about sharks | Audience: Age 4–7. | Includes bibliographical references and index.
Identifiers: LCCN 2018002871 (print) | LCCN 2018008475 (ebook) | ISBN 9781977101631 (eBook PDF) | ISBN 9781977101556 (hardcover) | ISBN 9781977101594 (paperback)
Subjects: LCSH: Oceanic whitetip shark—Juvenile literature.
Classification: LCC QL638.95.C3 (ebook) | LCC QL638.95.C3 R36 2019 (print) | DDC 597.3/4—dc23
LC record available at https://lccn.loc.gov/2018002871

Editorial Credits
Marissa Kirkman, editor; Charmaine Whitman, designer; Kelly Garvin, media researcher; Kathy McColley, production specialist

Image Credits
Alamy: Charles Hood, 9, David Fleetham, 17, Doug Perrine, 13; National Geographic Creative/Jim Abernathy, 19; Seapics/Eric Cheng, 15; Shutterstock: A Cotton Photo, 1, Brent Barnes, 7, Dray van Beeck, 21, James A Dawson, 5, martin_hristov, 11, Maquiladora, 10, Rich Carey, 3, 24, Shane Gross, cover, Willyam Bradbury, 23

Note to Parents and Teachers

The All About Sharks set supports national curriculum standards for science related to the characteristics and behavior of animals. This book describes and illustrates oceanic whitetip sharks. The images support early readers in understanding the text. The repetition of words and phrases helps early readers learn new words. This book also introduces early readers to subject-specific vocabulary words, which are defined in the Glossary section. Early readers may need assistance to read some words and to use the Table of Contents, Glossary, Read More, Internet Sites, Critical Thinking Questions, and Index sections of the book.

Printed and bound in China.
309

Table of Contents

A Forceful Hunter

A sneaky shark creeps through
the open ocean. It is on the hunt.
The shark charges into a school of tuna.
Chomp! The oceanic whitetip shark
grabs its meal.

Oceanic whitetip sharks swim in warm waters around the world. They stay mainly in the deep, open sea. Their habitat has plenty of food. They are strong ocean hunters.

Tip of the Fin

Oceanic whitetips have shiny gray-brown backs. They have white bellies. Their fins have white tips. The shark's coloring tricks prey. They think the shark is a school of fish.

Oceanic whitetips have powerful bodies with pointed snouts. Their dorsal fins are rounded. Their long pectoral fins help them glide as they swim.

5 feet (1.5 meters)

6.5–10 feet (2 to 3 meters)

dorsal fins

pectoral fins

Hunting and Eating

Oceanic whitetips eat whenever they get the chance. They are more bold than other sharks. They often scare other sharks away from food.

The oceanic whitetip's top teeth are jagged triangles. Its bottom teeth are smaller and more pointy. Snap! Their sharp teeth can grab fast-swimming fish.

Oceanic whitetips eat many things. They mainly hunt large fishes like tuna and marlins. They also catch octopuses, sea turtles, and seabirds.

Oceanic Whitetip Babies

Oceanic whitetip pups grow inside their mother.

One to 15 pups are born at a time.

Pups are 23 to 26 inches (60–65 centimeters) long at birth.

The young sharks are on their own. They grow into adults in about six to seven years. They may live for up to 22 years.

Glossary

dorsal fin—a fin located on the back

habitat—the natural place and conditions in which a plant or animal lives

hunt—to find and catch animals for food

marlin—a large, fast-swimming fish in the Atlantic ocean

pectoral fins—a pair of fins on each side of the head

prey—an animal hunted by another animal for food

pup—a young shark

school—a large number of the same kind of fish swimming and feeding together

snout—the long front part of an animal's head; it includes the nose, mouth, and jaws

Read More

Ellwood, Nancy and Parrish, Margaret. *Sharkpedia.* Second Edition. New York: DK Publishing, 2017.

Green, Sara. *The Oceanic Whitetip Shark.* Shark Fact Files. Minneapolis: Bellwether Media, 2013.

Meister, Cari. *Sharks.* Life under the Sea. Minneapolis: Jump!, 2014.

Internet Sites

FactHound offers a safe, fun way to find Internet sites related to this book. All of the sites on FactHound have been researched by our staff.

Here's all you do:

Visit *www.facthound.com*

Type in this code: 9781977101556

 Check out projects, games and lots more at **www.capstonekids.com**

Critical Thinking Questions

1. List three physical features of an oceanic whitetip shark.

2. How do an oceanic whitetip's pectoral fins help it swim?

3. Describe the two kinds of teeth an oceanic whitetip has. Why do you think they are different?

Index